HRyA

Black Achievement IN SCIENCE

Environmental Science

MC

Mason Crest

Black
Achievement
IN SCIENCE

Biology	Inventors
Chemistry	Medicine
Computer Science	Physics
Engineering	Space
Environmental Science	Technology

Black
Achievement
IN SCIENCE

Environmental Science

By JANE GARDNER

Foreword by Malinda Gilmore and Mel Poulson,
National Organization for the Advancement of
Black Chemists and Chemical Engineers

Mason Crest
450 Parkway Drive, Suite D
Broomall, PA 19008
www.masoncrest.com

© 2017 by Mason Crest, an imprint of National Highlights, Inc.

Printed and bound in the United States of America.

Series ISBN: 978-1-4222-3554-6
Hardback ISBN: 978-1-4222-3559-1
EBook ISBN: 978-1-4222-8326-4

First printing
1 3 5 7 9 8 6 4 2

Produced by Shoreline Publishing Group LLC
Santa Barbara, California
Editorial Director: James Buckley Jr.
Designer: Patty Kelley
Production: Sandy Gordon
www.shorelinepublishing.com

Cover photographs by Wavebreakmedia Ltd./Dreamstime.

Library of Congress Cataloging-in-Publication Data on file with the Publisher.

Contents

Key Icons to Look for

Words to Understand: These words with their easy-to-understand definitions will increase the reader's understanding of the text, while building vocabulary skills.

Research Projects: Readers are pointed toward areas of further inquiry connected to each chapter. Suggestions are provided for projects that encourage deeper research and analysis.

Text-Dependent Questions: These questions send the reader back to the text for more careful attention to the evidence presented here.

Series Glossary of Key Terms: This back-of-the-book glossary contains terminology used throughout this series. Words found here increase the reader's ability to read and comprehend higher-level books and articles in this field.

Educational Videos: Readers can view videos by scanning our QR codes, providing them with additional educational content to supplement the text. Examples include news coverage, moments in history, speeches, iconic moments, and much more!

Science, Technology, Engineering and Mathematics (STEM) are vital to our future, the future of our country, the future of our regions, and the future of our children. STEM is everywhere and it shapes our everyday experiences. Science and technology have become the leading foundation of global development. Both subjects continue to improve the quality of life as new findings, inventions, and creations emerge from the basis of science. A career in a STEM discipline is a fantastic choice and one that should be explored by many.

In today's society, STEM is becoming more diverse and even internationalized. However, the shortage of African Americans and other minorities, including women, still exists. This series—***Black Achievement in Science***—reveals the numerous career choices and pathways that great African-American scientists, technologists, engineers, and mathematicians have pursued to become successful in a STEM discipline. The purpose of this series of books is to inspire, motivate, encourage, and educate people about the numerous career choices and pathways in STEM. We applaud the authors for sharing the experiences of our forefathers and foremothers and ultimately increasing the number of people of color in STEM and, more

By Malinda Gilmore, NOBCChE Executive Board Chair and
Mel Poulson, NOBCChE Executive Board Vice-Chair

specifically, increasing the number of African Americans to pursue careers in STEM.

The personal experiences and accomplishments shared within are truly inspiring and gratifying. It is our hope that by reading about the lives and careers of these great scientists, technologists, engineers, and mathematicians, the reader might become inspired and totally committed to pursue a career in a STEM discipline and say to themselves, "If they were able to do it, then I am definitely able to do it, and this, too, can be me." Hopefully, the reader will realize that these great accomplishments didn't come easily. It was because of hard work, perseverance, and determination that these chosen individuals were so successful.

As Executive Board Members of The National Organization for the Professional Advancement of Black Chemists and Chemical Engineers (NOBCChE) we are excited about this series. For more than 40 years, NOBCChE has promoted the STEM fields and its mission is to build an eminent cadre of people of color in STEM. Our mission is in line with the overall purpose of this series and we are indeed committed to inspiring our youth to explore and contribute to our country's future in science, technology, engineering, and mathematics.

We encourage all readers to enjoy the series in its entirety and identify with a personal story that resonates well with you. Learn more about that person and their career pathway, and you can be just like them.

What is environmental science? There is a short answer and a much longer answer to this question. The short answer is that environmental science is concerned with the relationship between organisms (usually humans) and their surroundings. The longer answer is that environmental science is a branch of science concerned with the environment. It uses physical and biological sciences to identify and find solutions to environmental problems. Environmental science involves fields such as ecology, biology, geology, physics, chemistry, and atmospheric sciences. Environmental science started when people began to focus on natural sciences and medicine. Environmental science is more than just the study of the environment; it is the study of relationships and consequences and the future.

People who study environmental science come from all backgrounds and walks of life. As you will discover in this book, there are many ways to be concerned with the environment and work to make the world a better place. These scientists made contributions including revolutionizing farming practices to protect the soil and increase productivity. Others worked to bring science opportunities to disadvantaged youth in the US, while yet others spent their careers focusing on how drilling for oil in remote regions in Africa can impact the environment.

This book is part of a series highlighting the achievements of black scientists. As you will read, many of the environmental scientists in this book were met with opposi-

tion, hardships, and prejudice. The chemists introduced here range from George Washington Carver, who was born into slavery in the 1800s to Jerome Nriagu, who was born to a very poor family in Nigeria. Not only are these scientists notable for their scientific and educational accomplishments, but also for the social and personal obstacles they overcame in their pursuit of education and science. Most

Environmental scientists start with a base of love of the Earth and everything that grows.

of them were driven by a strong desire to improve the living conditions and health of underserved communities.

The scientists featured in this book came from all over the US and the world. Some gave back to society by heading government agencies designed to protecting the environment or by advising presidents and world leaders on environmental issues. Others became teachers, passing their infectious love of science on to generations of students. These scientists were, and are, more than simply scientists in lab coats. They are examples of how science can help others.

There are countless environmental scientists of all backgrounds, who have done amazing things and overcome obstacles. This is the story of only eight of them. Perhaps you will be inspired by their strength and determination to use their model for part of your own life. ●

Words to Understand

botany
the study of plant biology

pathology
the study of diseases and the changes they cause in organisms

Chapter 1

George Washington Carver

Born:
1864 (?))

Died:
1963

Nationality:
American

Achievements:
Botanist and chemist who found new uses for plants and inspired generations of black scientists

T he exact date of George Washington Carver's birth is uncertain. He was born a slave in Mississippi sometime around 1864. This was toward the end of the American Civil War and Carver's mother, Mary, was owned by Mr. Moses Carver. Carver's father was a slave owned by a neighbor, but he was killed in an accident before Carver was born. Carver and his mother were kidnapped when he was a baby. Their owner, Mr. Carver, hired someone to find Mary and her baby. Mary died under suspicious circumstances and only baby George was returned to the Carver home.

With the end of the Civil War and slavery in 1865, young Carver had a new home. Moses Carver and his wife, Susan, took him in and raised him. He was sickly as a young boy, and was not much help in the fields or

on the farm. He spent most of his time helping with household chores such as cooking, laundry, and sewing.

The Carvers taught George to read and write. As a result, he gained an appreciation for learning and a thirst for knowledge. George left the Carver home when he was young to go to a school for black children. Eventually, after attending several different schools, he graduated from Minneapolis High School in Kansas. He was accepted to Highland College but when he arrived on campus, he was asked to leave. The administrators did not realize he was black, and indicated that they did not accept students of his race. Several years later, he applied and was accepted to Iowa State Agricultural College in Ames.

Carver was interested in many things: music, art, botany, chemistry, and agriculture. He eventually decided to study **botany** and went on to earn both a bachelor of science degree and a masters' degree in plant **pathology** at Iowa State.

After Iowa State, he was hired by the great

Though slavery had ended in Carver's time, many blacks still farmed.

African-American educator Booker T. Washington to work and teach at Tuskegee Institute in Alabama. Carver worked there for many years and influenced several generations of students. He is probably best known for his work with the peanut. He discovered many new uses for the plant, some of which included nonfood uses. He worked with not only peanuts but also with sweet potatoes, soybeans, and pecans, inventing hundreds of products from these crops along the way, including plastics, dyes, and a form of gasoline.

Carver's studies of cotton helped farmers improve crops.

But Carver also made great contributions in the area of environmental science. His research and training led him to the conclusion that crop rotation was vital for some of the poorest farmers in the South, farmers who were primarily former slaves. Crop rotation is the practice of growing different crops in a field over successive years. At this time, many farmers relied heavily on planting cotton as their primary crop. However, doing so season after season decreased the fertility of the soil. A less fertile soil would not produce as many plants, which could lead to erosion and severely impact the productivity and yield of the farmers. The work that Carver did at Tuskegee suggested that planting other crops in a cotton field would increase the fertility of the soil and therefore increase the crop yield and decrease soil erosion.

In his later years, Carver was repeatedly honored by national and international groups for his pioneering work.

Carver introduced these farmers, whose backgrounds were mostly similar to his, to the idea of rotating the crops in a field seasonally. He also showed them alternative cash crops that they could grow on their fields. Cotton was, for a long time, the largest cash crop in the South, but with Carver's inventions using soybeans, sweet potatoes, and pecans, he created uses for other crops.

Carver thought a lot about nature and the role that humans play as they interact with nature. He believed that in the natural world everything is a part of the whole. He knew that nothing exists in isolation, that everything is connected. He believed that if we ignore that connection, then the effects could be disastrous. George was a very spiritual man. He believed that God spoke through the beauty of nature and the joy of creating.

The advancements in environmental science and botany that George contributed to science made him one of the most well known African Americans of his time. President

Theodore Roosevelt asked his advice on agriculture in the US. His fame extended beyond the United States. He was made a member of the British Royal Society of Arts in 1916. This was a rare honor for any American. Mahatma Gandhi, the leader of India, also sought his advice on agriculture and nutrition.

Carver used his status as a prominent scientist to advocate for more advances in agriculture and science, and to explore the possibilities of racial harmony. ●

George W. Carver:
Accomplished man of science

Words to Understand

NAACP
National Association for the Advancement of Colored People, a major African American organization

prevalent
common, normal or regular

sea ice
sea water that has recently been frozen that is not yet part of a solid mass of ice

Chapter 2

Warren Washington

Born:
1936

Nationality:
American

Achievements:
Climatologist who did key work in studying climate change; former chair of National Science Board

Warren Washington was born in Oregon in 1936. At that time in American history, much of the country was segregated; that is, laws and society kept black people and white people apart. Oregon, however, was one place where there was a pronounced lack of segregation. Many African Americans moved there during World War II to escape segregation and to seek a place where they could feel equal. This is not to say that Washington and his family did not face discrimination, but it was not as **prevalent** as it may have been in other parts of the country.

Education was very important in his family. His maternal grandmother, Bessie, was the first generation in her family to live outside of slavery. His grandfather owned a general store in Alabama. His father, Edwin Washington, was a college graduate and

worked as a waiter on the Union Pacific Railroad. Washington was one of five children. His family attended church where he sang in the choir. He was a member of the Boy Scouts and was vice president of the Junior **NAACP** at his high school.

From a very young age, his parents and teachers encouraged Wahington's curiosity and interest in science. Some people at his school thought he should go to business school, not a general college. However, a mentor who recognized his interest and strength in science and physics

Washington started his career in science after receiving a pair of degrees from Oregon State University in Corvallis, Oregon.

encouraged him to attend college. He studied physics at Oregon State University, where he was one of the few black students. He earned a bachelor's degree in physics in 1958 and a master's degree in meteorology from Oregon State in 1960.

Washington continued with his science education and attended Penn State University where he pursed a PhD in meteorology and completed his degree in 1964. Specifically, he looked at the way that physics relates to the atmosphere. His first job was with the National Center for Atmospheric Research (or NCAR). At the time, he was the first black scientist hired there.

At the NCAR, Washington quickly became a leader in the study of global warming. His research, over his long career, has involved developing computer models to look at the current state of the atmosphere and make projections about the future. One thing that made his research unique was the fact that he began to include data about the ocean. The ocean plays a very significant role in Earth's

The high-altitude clean air in Boulder, Colorado, makes an excellent site for the work of the National Center for Atmospheric Research.

climate. Washington's climate models included the ocean and **sea ice**. As he continued to gather data, he also included things such as water on Earth's surface and vegetation in his models. The results of his modeling have added significantly to scientists' understanding of climate and climate change on Earth.

Washington's career in science has been outstanding. He worked for Presidents Reagan, Carter, Bush, and Clinton and their initiatives to understand global climate. President Jimmy Carter appointed him to the Committee on Oceans and Atmospheres. In 1994, President Bill Clinton

In 2010, Washington received the National Medal of Science from President Obama for a career of research and public service.

appointed him Chair of the National Science Board for a six-year term and then reappointed him to another term as Chair before Clinton left office. As chair of this board, Washington was asked at one point about his opinion about sending astronauts back to the Moon and even farther, to Mars. He did not, however, agree to these proposals, citing budget concerns.

Another area of focus for Washington was the impact of climate change on the poor in America. In his role as a presidential advisor, he was asked about the impact global warming had on poor communities. He was able to point to the fact that climate change and global warming significantly impacted disasters like Hurricane Katrina. Hurricane Katrina struck the Gulf Coast of the US in 2005, severely affecting the poorer, often black communities, in areas such as New Orleans.

Warren Washington has been recognized for his contributions to science and to society in many different ways. He is a past president of the American Meteorological Society and has honorary degrees from Oregon State, Bates College, and the University of Massachusetts at Amherst. In 2010, President Barack Obama awarded him the Nation Medal of Science. Warren Washington is an example of how an interest in science and a strong motivation to help others can truly make a difference to society. ●

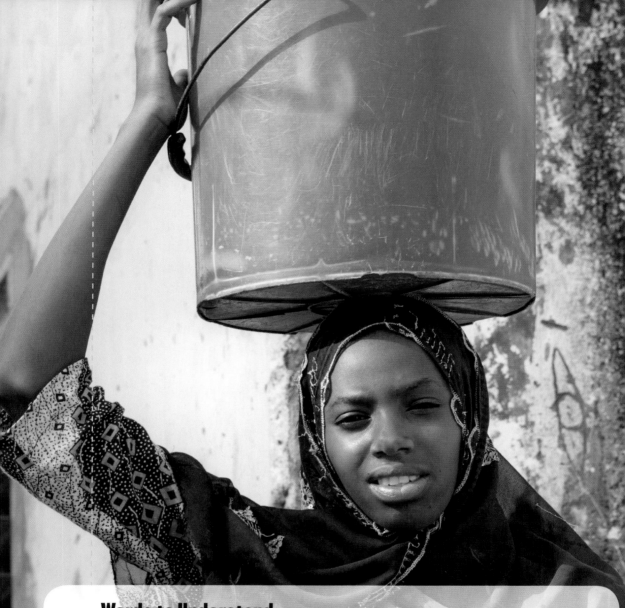

Words to Understand

geochemistry
a branch of geology that uses the principles of chemistry to study and describe phenomena that take place on Earth's surface and in Earth's waters

subsistence farming
the practice of growing or raising only what your family needs to survive

Chapter 3

Jerome Nriagu

Born:
1942

Nationality:
Nigerian

Achievements:
Chemist who has used his research to advocate for more work on clean air and water

I n 2012, when asked about his career by the Multicultural Environmental Leadership Development Initiative (MEDLI), Jerome Nriagu was quoted as saying, "helping communities solve their environmental problems is rewarding." Nriagu overcame significant odds to become a professor of environmental and industrial health at the University of Michigan.

Nriagu grew up in the western African nation of Nigeria. He was one of seven children and his parents were **subsistence farmers**. The life of a subsistence farmer is not always easy. Their focus is to grow enough food simply to feed their families. This might include food crops and the animals needed to feed and clothe the family for a year. Most of what is farmed is used by the family; occasionally, the excess might be sold at markets. A family

of nine people like Nriagu's would need to grow a lot of food and livestock.

At this time, companies were beginning to explore developing countries for oil and natural gas reserves. Nigeria was one such place. Unfortunately, little attention was paid to the environmental impact that the exploration and subsequent drilling for the resources could potentially have on the area. The problem was development that was becoming unregulated and unchecked.

Nriagu attended the University of Ibadan in Nigeria, located in the third largest city in that country. He stud-

Nriagu's home country of Nigeria exports a lot of oil, but did not carefully watch its environmental impact.

Working in Canada for many years, Nriagu helped the government work to keep the Great Lakes clean.

ied earth science as an undergraduate student and earned his bachelor's degree in 1965. Nriagu was sure he wanted to continue his study of earth science and geology and work at exploring for oil and gas in Nigeria. He received a scholarship to study petroleum geology at the University of Wisconsin in Madison. However, once there, he began to realize that he was more interested in focusing on the environmental impact that drilling would have on a developing country like Nigeria, than focusing on the drilling itself. He had seen how the unregulated drilling and exploration affected his country, and wanted to make a difference by working to solve some of the pollution problems associated with this unregulated development.

He changed his major to low-temperature **geochemistry**, or environmental chemistry, and earned his master's degree from the University of Wisconsin in 1967. He then moved

to the University of Toronto and earned a doctorate degree in environmental chemistry in 1970.

Nriagu began working for the National Water Resource Institute in Ontario, Canada, as a research scientist after completing his degree. For the next 20 years he worked there, conducting research to support the policies and programs set up to improve the water quality in the Great Lakes. He was next offered a position as a faculty member at the University of Michigan and is there today, as a professor of environmental health.

Nriagu's long career has given him the opportunity to speak out back home in Nigeria as well as worldwide.

As a professor, Nriagu has the opportunity to work with many different students and organizations. He teaches graduate level courses that focus on environmental health in developing countries, environmental chemistry, water quality, and issues of equality sorrowing environmental health. His research is centered mainly on looking at levels of toxic metals in the air, water, and soil. His other primary focus is on the question of environmental equity. His experiences in his home country of Nigeria had stuck with him and he set out to improve conditions for underserved communities in the United States and beyond. He served on several committees, giving expert testimony as a scientific advisor to organizations looking to study the environmental health effects of certain neighborhoods.

At the very heart of what he believes and what motivates him is a desire to work to improve living conditions for others. Jerome Nriagu works with the public interest on the forefront of his mind. He has been successful in his goal of reducing the impact of environmental hazards in the US, and around the world. ●

Words to Understand

urban planning
process that takes land use, the environment, the welfare of the citizens, and urban design into account as designs for transportation, housing, and commutations are planned

Chapter 4

Carl Anthony

Nationality:
American

Achievements:
**City planner and architect
who focuses on expanding
access to "green" space in
underserved urban areas**

Often our experiences as children shape our lives in the future. This was certainly the case for Carl Anthony. He put the experiences he had as a child growing up in Philadelphia (left) to a good use as he became an architect and urban planner later in life and focused on the questions surrounding race, poverty, and the environment. Anthony points to an experience he had as a third-grade student in the science club. At the time, he recalls feeling excluded when the club focused on topics such as dinosaurs, and stars, and even William Penn. He realized that issues that were relevant to him as a black student in an integrated elementary school and to his own community were not being discussed. He saw, even at a young age, how race and issues involving the environment can be very complicated.

The city of Philadelphia is known for its tradition of **urban planning**. Urban planning is a process that takes land use, the environment, the welfare of the citizens, and urban design into account as designs for transportation, housing, and commuting are mapped out. Anthony noticed, even as a child, that plans focused on working with the environment tended not to focus on the needs of black people and low-income regions of the city. These impressions stayed with him. His observations and ideas led him to seek for ways to combine the basic ideas of the Civil Rights Movement with architecture and urban planning.

While working in Harlem for ARCH, Anthony worked to call attention to underserved neighborhoods.

As a young adult, he began working with the Architecture Renewal Community in Harlem (ARCH), based in New York City. Many people at this time were beginning to approach architecture and design by considering the environment at the same time. ARCH was organized to address issues of social and economic justice in the Harlem neighborhood of New York City. While there, Anthony worked on the Neighborhood Commons Project, which converted vacant lots in a neighborhood into community parks and spaces.

Anthony's work encouraged clean parks near families in Manhattan.

The idea was to involve as many of the local residents as possible to help create and maintain these areas. As a result of this experience, Anthony decided to pursue architecture as a career and graduated in 1969 from Columbia University with a degree in architecture.

He began to question the direction that ARCH was taking and decided to go in another direction. In fact, he traveled to Africa to study the traditional architecture of African

cultures in hopes that he could incorporate some of what he saw into his own designs and work in the future.

After his time in Africa, Anthony began to teach at the University of California at Berkeley. His focus while there was on creating designs that were green—or environmentally friendly. He still was focused on working on issues facing poor communities, an idea that was met with little support from his colleges. He taught at Berkeley for ten years before leaving to work as an architect and planner in Oakland, California.

Even as he worked, Anthony felt removed from the communities he was interested in helping and lost many of his contacts there. As a result, he founded the Urban Habitat Program in 1989. This was a program dedicated to promoting environmental leadership in black communities to develop sustainable communities in the San Francisco Bay area. This experience led Anthony, along with a colleague named Luke Cole, to create a journal called *Race, Poverty, and Environment*. This journal provided articles and information

Anthony's work with the Ford Foundation encourages young people to get involved in the environment.

on looking at environmental issues and their relationship to race and poverty.

Anthony's career moved on to other organizations. He served as president of the Earth Island Institute and works now as the director of the Ford Foundation's Sustainable Metropolitan Communities Initiative. Social justice, environmental issues, and race and poverty have never been far from his mind. Carl Anthony has worked very hard to bring these issues to the forefront of many discussions. ●

A short speech by Carl Anthony

Words to Understand

doctorate
the highest level of postgraduate education

model
in this case, to create a virtual plan that predicts the design of a product or location of a substance

Chapter 5

Philip Emeagwali

Born:
1954

Nationality:
Nigerian

Achievements:
Engineer who works to use computer models to help his country by finding oil more safely

Environmental science is a wide-reaching discipline. Many, many disciplines can work to make advances that will protect and maintain the environment. There are the more obvious sciences such as geology, ecology, or biology. And then there are other studies, such as computer science, which can help advance our understanding of the environment. Dr. Philip Emeagwali is a computer scientist who is using his knowledge of some of the most sophisticated computer systems in the world to help advance our understanding of environmental science.

Emeagwali grew up in Nigeria in the 1950s and early 1960s. At that time, Nigeria was torn apart by civil war. The building his family lived in had been hit by rocket shells and crumbled around him. Like many African schoolchildren at the time, Emeagwali

dropped out of school at the age of 14. His father could not pay to continue with his formal education, but kept teaching him at home because he saw how much his son loved learning. Emeagwali would challenge himself by doing things like trying to solve 100 math problems in an hour. He knew that education was a way to better himself.

At 17, he earned a scholarship to Oregon State University. He graduated from there with a BS in mathematics. Emeagwali continued his education and eventually earned two master's degrees—one in environmental engineering and the other in applied mathematics. These may seem to be two very different disciplines, but in the years to come, his background in environmental studies and math served him well.

Emeagwali continued his education and was accepted in the University of Michigan's Civil Engineering **doctorate** program in 1987. When deciding upon a project for his doctoral research, Philip coupled his understanding of math and computers with an issue that was important to his home country of Nigeria. Nigeria has many reservoirs of oil, which were at that time, untapped. He realized that one of the biggest challenges facing the petroleum industry was the uncertainty surrounding the underground oil reserves. That is, you can't drill for oil unless you can find it underground. Emeagwali went to work, figuring out a way to get microprocessors working together to do more work than a super

Philip Emeagwali

The oil industry has created a lot of jobs in Nigeria. Emeagwali works to help with that, while also protecting the earth.

But he did not stop there. His use of hundreds and hundreds of microprocessors had many practical applications. Not only did he work on simulating the petroleum resources in the world but he also used the modeling power of the computers to work on predicting the weather. His advances in the world of computers helped expand our knowledge of the atmosphere. Emeagwali hopes that his work will be able to help forecast weather far into the future and help simulate the impacts of warming trends on the planet.

Emeagwali is an example of a scientist who may not be typically thought of as an environmental scientist. It was the application of his knowledge and understanding of math, engineering, and computers that have made his contribution to environmental science significant. Computer modeling of weather, weather patterns, and global climate change is vital to our understanding of the impact of global warming on the environment. Philip Emeagwali's contributions have gone a long way to helping future scientists work on these problems. ●

Words to Understand

trace elements
a sample that has an average concentration of fewer than 100 parts per million

Larry Robinson

Born:
1955

Nationality:
American

Achievements:
Environmental chemist with interest in trace elements who has become a key government official and longtime teacher

Larry Robinson has had an impressive career using his background in chemistry and environmental science to not only protect fragile coastal ecosystems, but also to help solve a century-old mystery—the death of President Zachary Taylor.

Robinson received a BS in chemistry from Memphis State University in 1979, graduating with honors. He then earned a doctorate degree in nuclear chemistry from Washington University in St. Louis in 1984. His first job after graduation was at Oak Ridge National Laboratory (ORNL) in Tennessee. ORNL is the largest laboratory focused on science and energy and is run by the US Department of Energy. The research conducted there is diverse, but mostly focuses in some way on scientific problems concerned with energy or security. Four main areas of science and technology that scientists

and engineers at ORNL focus on are neutrons, computers, material science, and nuclear processes. Robinson joined the nuclear research group there in 1984 and worked as a group leader until he left in 1997.

Environmental chemistry, specifically the detection of **trace elements** in the environment, has been one of his main career focuses. Typically, he looks for trace elements in the environment from nuclear sources. But this knowledge also led him to a very high-profile investigation into the death of President Zachary Taylor in 1850.

Environmental chemists study plants, to find out how they are affected by climate and other factors.

President Taylor was in office for just over a year when he suddenly became ill. On July 4, 1850, he attended celebrations at the Washington Monument, which was under construction at that time. While there he reportedly ate raw fruit and ice milk. He soon became ill with an unknown digestive issue. His doctors tried to treat him the best they could but their efforts failed. He became sicker and sicker and died on July 9, 1850. Many felt Taylor's death was suspicious and some accused pro-slavery Southerners of poisoning the president.

Robinson played chemical detective while looking at Pres. Zachary Taylor.

Questions about his death remained for more than 100 years. Descendants of President Taylor agreed to have his body exhumed and hair and fingernail samples analyzed. Robinson was part of a team of researchers who analyzed those samples for trace elements. He and his colleagues used a High Flux Isotope reactor at ORNL to try to identify and measure arsenic levels in the samples. They concluded that if President Taylor had been poisoned, it was not by arsenic. The levels of arsenic in the samples were much lower than would be expected of someone who was poisoned. The true cause of death of President Zachary Taylor still remains a mystery.

As one of the leaders of NOAA, Robinson (right) often joined other experts in doing field research.

In 1997, Robinson was offered a faculty position at Florida A & M University (FAMU) in Tallahassee. His research there focused on environmental chemistry of coastal ecosystems. His role at FAMU expanded, and he eventually became director of the Environmental Sciences Institute there. He expanded course and degree offerings to include new BS and PhD programs. He became the provost and vice president for academic affairs at the university in 2003 and then again years later in 2012.

Robinson left FAMU in 2010 to become the assistant secretary of commerce in the National Oceanic and Atmospheric Administration (NOAA). NOAA was tasked with protecting, restoring, and managing the use of ocean and coastal resources. Robinson was hired to help guide the policy and programs to this goal. As assistant secretary, he managed and oversaw programs designed to protect marine fisheries, sanctuaries, and nautical charts. When he accepted the position at NOAA, he said "As we confront climate change and other threats to our coastal communities, I look forward to helping develop and implement national ocean policy, and work with fishing communities and councils around the country to effectively manage our valuable fisheries."

Larry Robinson returned to FAMU in 2011 as a professor. He capped off his long career in academics when was appointed the interim president of the university in 2012. He served until 2014, when a permanent president was chosen and he returned to his classroom and his continuing studies. ●

Words to Understand

climate change
change in global weather patterns over an extended period of time

contentious
in dispute; causing controversy

greenhouse gases
gases in the atmosphere, such as carbon dioxide, water vapor, methane, and ozone, which absorb heat from the Sun and warm Earth's surface

Lisa Perez Jackson

Born:
1962

Nationality:
American

Achievements:
Chemist who worked to clean up toxic waste sites and then became government agency leader

The United States Environmental Protection Agency, or EPA, is tasked with protecting human health and the environment. This is accomplished by writing and enforcing the laws passed by the US Congress. The EPA oversees the quality of our soil and air, offers suggestions about reducing the release of greenhouse gases to slow climate change, and sets regulations to protect the environment. The head of this very important organization has a significant role in the government and in people's lives. Lisa P. Jackson served as the head of the EPA from 2009–2013. Her path to this important role was an interesting one.

Lisa Jackson was born in Pennsylvania in 1962. A few weeks later, she was adopted by a family from Louisiana. She grew up in a middle-class neighborhood in New Orleans called Pontchartrain Park, which was home

Jackson got her start helping in New Orleans, which can often be hit with floods that cause great damage.

to many African-America families. Her father worked in the post office and her mother was a secretary. She and her family were not poor, but she was aware of the poverty and poor living conditions that many people in New Orleans faced.

The city of New Orleans has many canals as well as oil drilling facilities. It is susceptible to flooding during storms. As Jackson grew up, she came to realize that many of the people in New Orleans, especially those who were poor and underprivileged, were being affected by the physical conditions in the city.

Jackson attended an all-girls Catholic school called St. Mary's Dominican High School, where she was valedictorian of her class, and received a scholarship to attend Tulane University in New Orleans. She majored in chemical engineering and was one of the few black women in her class at

Tulane. Jackson worked hard in college, and was not happy unless she was excelling in her studies. She graduated with honors from Tulane in 1983 and went to graduate school at Princeton University. She completed a master's degree in chemical engineering there in 1986.

After graduation, Jackson spent the next two years working for a nonprofit organization called Clean Sites, Inc. Clean Sites worked to manage environmental clean-up projects. Many of those projects were part of the Superfund program. The Superfund or Comprehensive Environmental Response, Compensation, and Liability Act is a law passed in the US in 1980 to clean up areas contaminated with hazardous materials and substances. This experience with Superfund projects opened doors for Jackson and she was able to get a job with the Environmental Protection Agency's Superfund program as a staff engineer.

Her next professional move was to fill a position at the Department of Environmental Protection (DEP) for the state of New Jersey. She was soon the commissioner of this organization. In this position she used her background in science and engineering, but had to become very involved in politics as well. As a government

A Superfund site is designated by the government to receive intensive cleanup efforts.

agency, the DEP was tasked with dealing with environmental problems, but making that happen can sometimes become **contentious** and political. Jackson thrived, however, and led her agency well.

In 2008, President-elect Barack Obama nominated Jackson as administrator of the EPA. With her appointment in 2009, she became the first African American to head the agency. When appointed, she pledged to focus on the core issues inherent in the EPA's mission—protecting air and water quality, preventing exposure to toxic contamination,

Jackson (right) was part of President Obama's key advisory team as the nation responded to a major 2010 oil spill.

and reducing greenhouse gases. She set priorities of focusing on certain groups—children, the elderly, and low-income communities. She pointed out that those groups are often most susceptible to health and environmental threats.

During her tenure as head of the EPA, Jackson set out plans to make many drastic improvements to the environment. For example, she called for stricter limits on the National Ambient Air Quality Standards and served as chair on the Gulf Coast Ecosystem Restoration Task Force after the 2010 Deepwater Horizon oil spill. Jackson was also very vocal about her concerns surrounding controversial projects such as the Keystone Pipeline and amending EPA's ability to regular greenhouse gas emissions. She resigned from the EPA in 2013, and it is believed that she did so because she was concerned that President Obama would support the Keystone pipeline and she did not want that to happen while she was head of the EPA. (As it turned out, Obama did not approve the pipeline in late 2015, though the discussion about this cross-national oil system continues.)

Lisa Perez Jackson currently works for Apple, Inc., and oversees their environmental issues. ●

Lisa Perez Jackson on Apple's investments in clean energy

Words to Understand

effluent
runoff from a stream or river

seining
fishing using a seine—a net that hangs vertically in the water with its bottom edge held down by weights and its top edge held up by floats

Chapter 7

Nkrumah Frazier

Born:
1954

Nationality:
American

Achievements:
Scientist and community
activist focused on
encouraging stewardship
and outdoor activity

Are you curious about the world around you? Would you like to think that you could make a difference? Perhaps there is something you can do. A group you could join, or a cause you could take up. This is very similar to what Nkrumah Frazier has done. His approach to his life and career has been to surround himself with the topics he is passionate about and work to encourage others to become just as passionate about them.

Frazier grew up on a farm in the southern part of Mississippi. He and his brother spent their time exploring the woods and fields on their farm and beyond. His family had gardens where they grew their own vegetables and owned cows as well. His father taught him to hunt, but not for sport. From a young age, Frazier was taught to only take enough for his family's needs. The idea of working

with nature and the environment was important to him from his young days.

Growing up, Frazier knew he wanted to either be a scientist or work with animals. He chose to study environmental biology in college. In 2009, he earned a bachelor's degree in environmental biology from the University of Southern Mississippi in Hattiesburg. He put that education to work in an environmental laboratory where he held the

Like many environmental scientists, Frazier splits his time between work in the field and time in the lab.

position of lab technician. Frazier spent many hours each day collecting and testing water samples. The lab was particularly concerned with whether or not the **effluent**, or liquid runoff, was contaminated with materials that could prove to be toxic to fish or smaller invertebrates in the environment.

Inspiring kids to become garden-lovers is part of Frazier's mission.

Frazier never forgot his dream of working with animals either. He left the lab to work as an animal keeper at the Hattiesburg Zoo. This experience proved to be rewarding in many ways. Frazier has tried to follow the paths that interest him. It is important for people to keep their goals and dreams in sight as they grow and shape themselves as adults.

He returned to the biology department at the University of Southern Mississippi as a biology research technician. There he works on projects studying the fish along the Gulf Coast of Mississippi. Using techniques such as **seining** and trawling, he and his team catch the fish for study and cata-

logue them. In a 2013 interview, Frazier said that he got to "see things that men who have been fishing the waters their entire lives have never seen before."

With a diverse background in biology, environmental science, and an interest in animals, Frazier continued to want to give back to the community. He has become very active in many organizations intended to promote education and love of the environment. Spending time outside and with family and friends was part of his experiences growing up, and this is what he has spent years trying to cultivate for his

Frazier often leads groups of youngsters on trail walks, such as here at Mississippi's Black Creek Wilderness.

own daughters. For example, Frazier served as the co-chair of the Let's G.O. Outside Initiative focused on encouraging groups of people, of all ages, to connect with nature. He was a team member of Outdoor Afro, an organization dedicated to encouraging black people in the community to get out and participate in nature. Most recently, Frazier founded a group called Hikes Across America! to encourage groups around the country to sponsor hiking events. That might be in a city park or a vast forest land, spending time understanding more about nature, our role in nature, and how we can improve our lives by being part of nature.

Nkrumah Frazier has had a great career thus far. He has taken an educational background in environmental science, a love of nature, and a desire to be outside and used these to help and encourage others. Spreading the word about protecting the environment and living as part of the environment are vital to creating a world we can all live in for many generations to come. ●

Chapter 8

Careers in Environmental Science

If you like nature and the idea of helping to preserve it for future generations, then environmental science might be for you. Or maybe you have an interest in science in general and can see how there are many different applications that can work toward making the world a better place. Chemistry, biology, physics, geology—these are all great avenues to explore if you are interested in environmental science.

People who pursue a career in environmental science share some qualities, as you have seen in this book. They tend to be problem solvers, looking at a health or environmental problem and searching for a cause or a solution. Perhaps people fishing in a small lake notice deformities in a certain species of fish. They may rely on an environmental scientist with a background in biology to

identify the deformity and how it affects the fish. Another environmental scientist with a background in water quality or toxins may examine the water flowing into the lake to determine any sources of contamination. A team of people may be tasked to solve this particular problem.

Environmental scientists are researchers as well. Many environmental scientists may work in the field, or in a laboratory setting, gathering data to understand what is happening in the world around us. An environmental soil scientist may gather samples in the field and then analyze these samples for a variety of things in a laboratory. This data that is gathered will then be compared to data that others have gathered over the years and analyzed.

In the lab or in the field, environmental science is clearly a growing career field.

Research into past environmental issues and potential causes is often done. Environmental scientists often share their data and their findings at academic or professional meetings and conferences. There are many scientific and professional journals that environmental scientists read and contribute to. Many projects that environmental scientists are involved with are funded by grants offered by government agencies or corporations. A background in writing and grant writing would be useful to students of any science.

A person looking to work in the field of environmental science also needs a strong background in science and mathematics. Biology, physics, chemistry, or earth science would be options. Other disciplines include those in health care, policy making, and statistics.

As an environmental scientist, you could expect to work in a variety of locations. You may work in the field gathering samples or data. This may be in an urban park or in the deepest rainforest in the Amazon. Environmental scientists also work in the lab, analyzing samples and gathering data. Environmental scientists may serve as advisors to government agencies or corporations looking to understand the changes in the environment or to reduce their impact.

You probably won't work alone. Collaboration is important in this field. Often teams of scientists work together to create a plan to prevent, or control or remediate an existing environmental problem. Being able to work in a team setting is important.

There are many options open to you if you are interested in a career in environmental science. Consider this: it is predicted that employment opportunities in the area of environmental science will grow 15 percent from now until the year 2022, which is faster than average for all occupations. The public interest in issues such as global warming, alternative fuels, and oil extraction has focused much effort and attention on the environment. Might this be a career for you? ●

Text-Dependent Questions

1. What is crop rotation and how does it help farmers grow more food?

2. What is urban planning and how does it affect the environment?

3. How did Carl Anthony's expertise in meteorology help his work with the environment?

4. What are some of the roles of the Environmental Protection Agency?

5. For what national organization did Larry Robinson work? What are some of the goals of that organization?

6. Which of the subjects in this book was a two-term president of the National Science Board?

7. Other than peanuts, what products did George Washington Carver work with?

Suggested Research Projects

Have these stories inspired you? Does the idea of being an environmental scientist interest you? Here are some ideas for topics you could explore in more depth.

1. Jerome Nriagu came from a family of subsistence farmers. How much food and livestock would it take to feed your family for a month? Start a list of the food your family eats in a day, in a week, and in a month. Pay special attention to the amount of fruits, vegetables, meat, eggs, and dairy products. How much does your family waste or throw out? How do you think this would change if you were to grow your own food and raise your own livestock?

2. Helping connect people with nature has become one of the foundations of Nkrumah Frazier's professional career. What opportunities exist in your community? Check out organizations in your school or city that allow you to interact with nature and help preserve open space.

3. Green buildings and green architecture are hot topics right now. Carl Anthony spends much of his time and effort designing communities and buildings. Find out more about green buildings and the LEED certification process at the website of the US Green Building Council. http://www.usgbc.org/LEED/. See if there are LEED certified buildings in your neighborhood.

Find Out More

Websites

meldi.snre.umich.edu
The Multicultural Environmental Leadership Development initiative is a great resource for learning more about environmental science and black scientists.

www.environmentalscience.org
Are you interested in environmental science but are just not sure where to start? Try this website. There are many resources here as well as information for people looking to study environmental science or get a job in the industry.

www2.epa.gov/learn-issues
The US EPA has a great website with many resources. Check out this site—it introduces the reader to a variety of issues facing our environment today and in the future.

www.nobcche.org/
Read about this organization run by the authors of the foreword of this book.

Books

Pennybacker, Mindy. *Do One Green Thing: Saving the Earth Through Simple, Everyday Choices*. New York: St. Martin's Griffin, 2010

Rodger, Ellen. *Reducing Your Foodprint: Farming, Cooking, and Eating for a Healthy Planet*. New York: Crabtree Publishing, 2010.

Sullivan, Otha Richard. *Black Stars: African American Women Scientists and Inventors*. Hoboken, NJ: Wiley, 2009.

Series Glossary of Key Terms

botany the study of plant biology

electron a negatively charged particle in an atom

genome all the DNA in an organism, including all the genes

nanometer a measurement of length that is one-billionth of a meter

nanotechnology manipulation of matter on an atomic or molecular scale

patent a set of exclusive rights granted to an inventor for a limited period of time in exchange for detailed public disclosure of an invention

periodic table the arrangement of all the known elements into a table based on increasing atomic number

protein large molecules in the body responsible for the structure and function of all the tissues in an organism

quantum mechanics the scientific principles that describe how matter on a small scale (such as atoms and electrons) behaves

segregated separated, in this case by race

ultraviolet a type of light, usually invisible, that can cause damage to the skin

Index

Photo credits

About the Author

Jane P. Gardner is the author of more than 30 books for young and young-adult readers on science and other nonfiction topics. She earned a master's degree in geology and a master's degree in education and also has years of experience teaching and developing science curriculum. In addition to writing, Jane also teaches science classes (including chemistry) at North Shore Community College. She lives in Massachusetts with her husband and their two sons.